J
358.4
COO   Cooper, Jason

       U.S. Air Force

DUE DATE

Haltom City Public Library
3201 Friendly Lane
Haltom City, TX 76117

U.S. AIR FORCE

FIGHTING FORCES

JASON COOPER

Rourke

Publishing LLC

Vero Beach, Florida 32964

www.rourkepublishing.com

PHOTO CREDITS: All photos courtesy of U.S. Air Force except pp 13, 25, 26, 27, 28 courtesy of National Archives.

Title page: *An HH-60G rescue helicopter prepares to pick up an Air Force pararescue team during a training mission.*

Editor: Frank Sloan

Cover and page design by Nicola Stratford

Library of Congress Cataloging-in-Publication Data

Cooper, Jason, 1942-
  U.S. Air Force / Jason Cooper.
     v. cm. — (Fighting forces)
Includes bibliographical references and index.
Contents: What the U.S. Air Force does — The U.S. Air Force at work — The Air Force Command — Life in the Air Force — Air Force weapons — The beginnings of the Air Force.
  ISBN 1-58952-712-7 (hardcover)
  1. United States. Air Force—Juvenile literature. [1. United States. Air Force.] I. Title. II. Series: Cooper, Jason, 1942- Fighting Forces
  UG633.C673 2003
  358.4'00973—dc21

                                        2003005286

Printed in the USA

CG/CG

TABLE OF
CONTENTS

WHAT THE U.S. AIR FORCE DOES

The Air Force is the American **armed service** most active in the air and in space. It is also the youngest of America's armed services. The nation's Army, Navy, Coast Guard, and Marine Corps were started in the late 1700s. The Air Force started much more recently. After all, there were no airplanes until 1903! The Air Force used to be part of the U.S. Army. It was known as the Army Air Corps. The Air Force became a separate service in 1947.

The warplanes and weapons of the Air Force help ▶
make it the most powerful air force on earth.

For all its youth, the Air Force has grown up quickly. Its rockets and **warheads** are among the most powerful weapons on earth. And Air Force satellites give America an important place in space.

Today the Air Force has about 350,000 men and women on active duty. Nearly 200,000 more serve in the Air Force **Reserve** and the Air National Guard. The Air Force also has about 150,000 **civilian** workers.

◀ *An Air Force sergeant inspects a missile inside its silo near Grand Forks Air Force Base, North Dakota.*

THE U.S. AIR FORCE AT WORK

Like other American armed services, the U.S. Air Force has been made powerful to prevent war. But if war begins, the Air Force can attack an enemy with a variety of powerful weapons. Some of them can be fired or carried over amazing distances. Others, like the so-called "smart" bombs, can be dropped with great accuracy. The Air Force can quickly reach enemy targets in the air, on land, and on the sea.

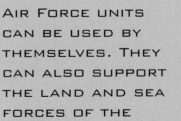

FACT FILE ★

AIR FORCE UNITS CAN BE USED BY THEMSELVES. THEY CAN ALSO SUPPORT THE LAND AND SEA FORCES OF THE ARMY, NAVY, AND MARINES.

The Air Force is the nation's defense against being attacked by air. The Air Force has several systems that can give early warning of an air attack.

▲ *The USAF's SR-71B, nicknamed the Blackbird, is a high-flying spy plane.*

The Air Force has another important job. It gathers important information about what enemy nations are doing. The Air Force calls this information **intelligence**. Intelligence is gathered by airplanes and satellites that are spies in the sky. They carry cameras and other instruments. The photos taken by an American U-2 spy plane in 1962 showed that Russia had put missiles into Cuba. The photos gave the United States proof of what Russia was doing. The United States then forced Russia to take its missiles home.

Workers watch a C-130 Hercules land. The Hercules ▶ *is delivering food supplies to Wajir, Kenya.*

Air Force power is used in other ways, too. The Air Force, for instance, works closely with the National Air and Space Administration (NASA). NASA is the organization that directs America's space programs.

During World War II (1939-45), U.S. bombers dropped bombs on much of Germany. These bombs helped to end the war. But just a few years later, the same bombers were called on to bring aid to the recently defeated Germans.

In June, 1948, Russia closed off all roads to West Berlin, Germany. Berliners had no incoming food or supplies. American and British planes, however, delivered more than 2 million tons (1.8 metric tons) of supplies. The "Berlin Airlift" was a huge success.

In more recent years, the U. S. Air Force has flown supplies to other needy people, such as those in Afghanistan and Iraq.

An Army Air Force B-17 bombs an airplane plant in Marienburg, Germany, in 1943. ▶

THE AIR FORCE COMMAND

U.S. armed services are under the overall command of civilians. Even the highest ranking Air Force generals have civilian bosses. One of those bosses is the secretary of the Air Force. Another is the secretary of Defense. Their boss is the commander-in-chief of all the armed services. That is the president of the United States.

The Air Force is run by the Department of the Air Force. That department is part of the U.S. Government's Department of Defense. The Department of Defense manages the Air Force, Army, Navy, and Marine Corps.

HIGHEST RANKS
IN DESCENDING ORDER
GENERAL
LIEUTENANT GENERAL
MAJOR GENERAL
BRIGADIER GENERAL
COLONEL
LIEUTENANT COLONEL
MAJOR
CAPTAIN
FIRST LIEUTENANT
SECOND LIEUTENANT

▲ *Very few airmen can become part of an Air Force Special Operations Squadron. Here two members of Air Force Special Operations take cover in a hangar during a training exercise against chemical attack.*

LIFE IN THE AIR FORCE

Like other armed services, the Air Force divides its men and women into two large groups: officers and **enlisted**. Officers have a higher rank and receive more pay than enlisted members. Officers also make more decisions.

Most men and women who join the Air Force have six weeks of basic training at Lackland Air Force Base, Texas. After basic training, they usually attend an Air Force school. There they learn a special skill. Young people who join the Air Force agree to stay in the service for four to six years.

The first 10 female officers to graduate from the Air Force Undergraduate Pilot Training Program pose in front of a T-38 training jet in 1977. ▶

The U.S. Air Force Academy in Colorado Springs, Colorado, is the Air Force's own officer training college. About 1,000 young men and women graduate as Air Force officers from the academy each year. They have agreed to serve an additional five years in the Air Force. Many go on to long Air Force careers.

AIR FORCE WEAPONS

   The U.S. Air Force has more than 40 different kinds of airplanes and helicopters. Each has a special use or several uses. Many of these aircraft are designed to fire guns and missiles. Some drop bombs. Others are used to carry fuel, soldiers, or equipment.

   Air Force fighter and attack jets can destroy enemy aircraft, ships, or ground forces. These are fast, sleek planes with one or two pilots. The F-15C and E Eagle fighters, for example, can fly about 1,875 miles (3,000 kilometers) per hour. The Air Force's F-117A Nighthawk attack jet carries weapons guided by **lasers**. The Nighthawk is one of the Air Force's "stealth" aircraft. It is designed to fool enemy **radar**. Radar is a system that finds flying objects long before anyone can see or hear them.

▲ *An F-117A Nighthawk stealth fighter refuels from an air tanker in midair.*

The twin-engine Thunderbolt flies at fairly low speed. Its job is to fly low and fire weapons to protect ground forces.

The C-17 Globemaster is the newest of the Air Force cargo planes. Cargo planes load up with freight.

The B-2 Spirit is the newest of the Air Force bombers. It is also a stealth aircraft. The B-1B Lancer is a fast bomber with adjustable wings.

◀ *A pair of two-engined A-10A Thunderbolts roars over a target practice area in Alaska.*

▲ *The B-52 stealth bomber is the latest in a long line of USAF bombers.*

The amazing B-52 bombers began to join the Air Force in 1955. They can fly higher and faster than most passenger jets. The Air Force has made steady improvements in its B-52s to keep them modern. B-52s dropped many of the bombs the Air Force used on Iraq during the 1991 Persian Gulf War.

Missiles are other important weapons. The Air Force has several types. Some can be fired from airplanes at other airplanes or at ground targets. Another type of missile is fired from the ground. The biggest and most powerful of these are called ICBMs (Intercontinental Ballistic Missiles). They can fly nearly 10,000 miles (16,000 kilometers) from one continent to another.

THE BEGINNINGS OF THE AIR FORCE

The Wright Brothers made the first flight with a motor-driven airplane in 1903. President Theodore R. Roosevelt took notice. He wanted the government to buy planes in 1907. And just two years later the government did buy an airplane. But the idea of air power for war did not catch on right away.

When World War I (1914-1918) began, the European powers already had hundreds of warplanes. America's Army Air Force, however, had only five. The United States entered World War I with no combat-ready planes in 1917. Still, two Americans, General Billy Mitchell and Eddie Rickenbacker, earned fame from the air war in Europe.

October 18, 1918, Eddie Rickenbacker with the Spad fighter plane he flew against the Germans in France. World War I would end just 24 days later. ▶

American General Billy Mitchell was in charge of hundreds of English and French planes. He believed that air power would be important to the future of America's defense.

Eddie Rickenbacker was America's first "ace." An ace is a pilot who shoots down five or more enemy aircraft. Rickenbacker shot down 22 planes and 4 spy balloons.

In World War II (1939-1945), air power was extremely important. General Henry "Hap" Arnold helped the American Army Air Force quickly become the world's most powerful air force. By war's end it had more than 2 million people in uniform and 80,000 airplanes!

American planes and their brave pilots helped destroy Japan's navy and air force in the Pacific. In Europe, Army Air Force bombers destroyed German factories, oil fields, cities, and much of the German Air Force. American planes destroyed 40,000 enemy aircraft. They had also dropped more than 2 million tons (1.8 metric tons) of bombs.

▲ *A B-25 bomber, one of the Mitchells named for the famous American general, takes off from the deck of the aircraft carrier* Hornet.

In August, 1945, an Army Air Force B-29 bomber dropped atomic bombs on Hiroshima and Nagasaki, Japan. The horrible damage caused by those two bombs forced Japan to surrender.

▲ *Smoke rises 12 miles (19 kilometers) after an American B-29 bomber dropped an atomic bomb on Nagasaki, Japan, in August, 1945.*

General Billy Mitchell had been right about air power. A World War II bomber, the B-25 Mitchell, was named for him. In 1946, 10 years after his death, he was honored with the nation's highest **military** award, the Congressional Medal of Honor. And Milwaukee's Mitchell Field airport is named in his honor.

In 1947, the Air Force became a separate armed service. Three years later it was in combat in the Korean War (1950-1953).

▲ *American F-86 fighter jets line up for combat flights in Korea, June, 1951.*

▲ *A YF-22 stealth fighter streaks over the western United States during a test flight. This is one of the latest, high-tech U.S. Air Force aircraft.*

In Korea, fighter jets fought against fighter jets for the first time. American planes shot down about 900 enemy planes in Korea with a loss of fewer than 150 of their own.

During the Vietnam War (1957-1975) American bombers were in action over Southeast Asia. The Air Force was again in action during the Persian Gulf War. In March and April, 2003, the Air Force played an important role in the war against Iraq.

The Air Force has a huge research program. Engineers and scientists, as well as pilots, are working to keep America's Air Force flying high.

GLOSSARY

armed service (AHRMD SER vuss) — any one of the military forces of a government, such as the U.S. Air Force

civilian (SUH vill yun) — one who is not a member of the armed forces

enlisted (EN LIST ud) — having joined one of the armed forces

intelligence (in TELL uh jence) — information gathered about an enemy force by spying

lasers (LAY zuhrz) — devices that make a very powerful beam of light

military (MILL uh tare ee) — having to do with or being part of the nation's armed forces

radar (RAY DAHR) — a system of radio beams through which objects in flight can be discovered before they are seen

reserve (REE ZURV) — the non-active soldiers who may be called to active duty in a national emergency

warheads (WOHR HEDZ) — explosive charges at the tip, or head, of a missile or rocket

INDEX

FURTHER READING

Alagna, Magdalena. *Life Inside the Air Force Academy*. Children's Press, 2002
Langley, Wanda. *The Air Force in Action*. Enslow, 2001

WEBSITE TO VISIT

www.af.mil

ABOUT THE AUTHOR

Jason Cooper has written several children's books about a variety of topics for Rourke Publishing, including the recent series *Eye to Eye with Big Cats* and *Holiday Celebrations*.